Pebble® Plus

T0081403

Life Around the World

Birthdays in Many Cultures

Revised Edition

by Martha E. H. Rustad

Consulting Editor: Gail Saunders-Smith, PhD

CAPSTONE PRESS
a capstone imprint

Pebble Plus is published by Capstone Press,
1710 Roe Crest Drive, North Mankato, Minnesota 56003.
www.mycapstone.com

Copyright © 2008, 2016 by Capstone Press, a Capstone imprint. All rights reserved.
No part of this publication may be reproduced in whole or in part, or stored in a retrieval system, or transmitted in any form or by any means, electronic, mechanical, photocopying, recording, or otherwise, without written permission of the publisher. For information regarding permission, write to Capstone Press,
1710 Roe Crest Drive, North Mankato, Minnesota 56003.

Library of Congress Cataloging-in-Publication Data is available on the Library of Congress website.
ISBN: 978-1-5157-4291-3 (hardback)
ISBN: 978-1-5157-4240-1 (paperback)
ISBN: 978-1-5157-4360-6 (ebook pdf)

Editorial Credits
Sarah L. Schuette, editor; Kim Brown, book designer; Alison Thiele, set designer; Wanda Winch, photo researcher

Photo Credits
Alamy: Cultura Creative, 11, david hancock, 5, Edwin Remsberg, 7; Capstone Studio: Karon Dubke, cover, 1; Getty Images: Niedring/Drentwett, 9; iStockphoto: Denisfilm, 13; Newscom: VARLEY/SIPA, 15; Shutterstock: Rabus Carmen Olga, 19, XiXinXing, 21; The Image Works, 17

Note to Parents and Teachers

The Life around the World set supports national social studies standards related to culture and geography. This book describes and illustrates birthdays in many cultures. The images support early readers in understanding the text. The repetition of words and phrases helps early readers learn new words. This book also introduces early readers to subject-specific vocabulary words, which are defined in the Glossary section. Early readers may need assistance to read some words and to use the Table of Contents, Glossary, Read More, Internet Sites, and Index sections of the book.

Printed in the United States 6024

Table of Contents

Birthday Parties 4
More Birthday Fun. 12
Your Birthday 20

Glossary 22
Internet Sites. 23
Read More 23
Index 24

Birthday Parties

People celebrate
their birthdays
in many cultures.

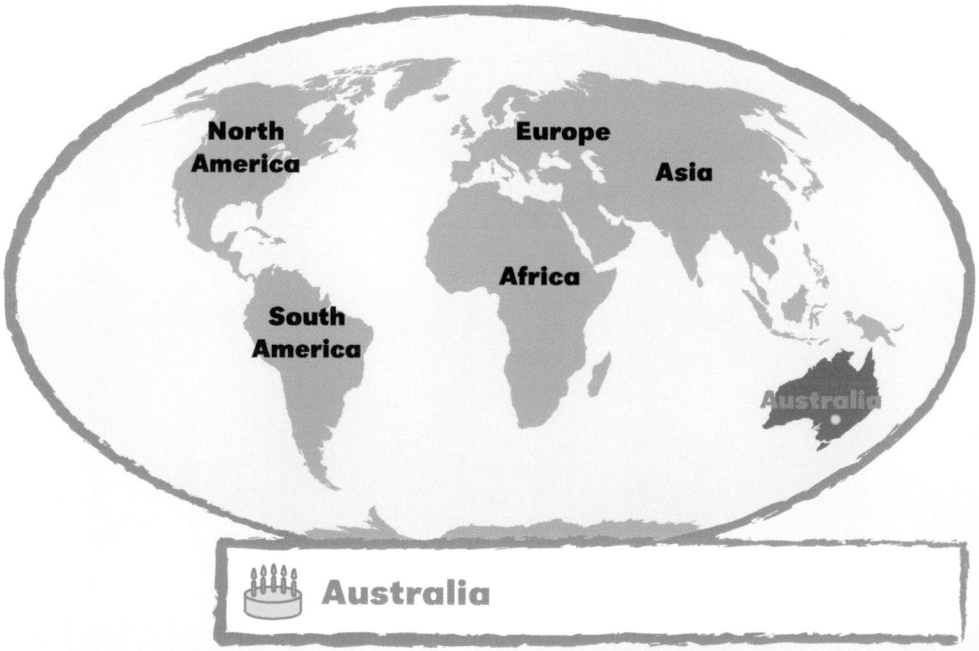

People play games
on their birthdays.
A girl in Mexico
breaks open a piñata.

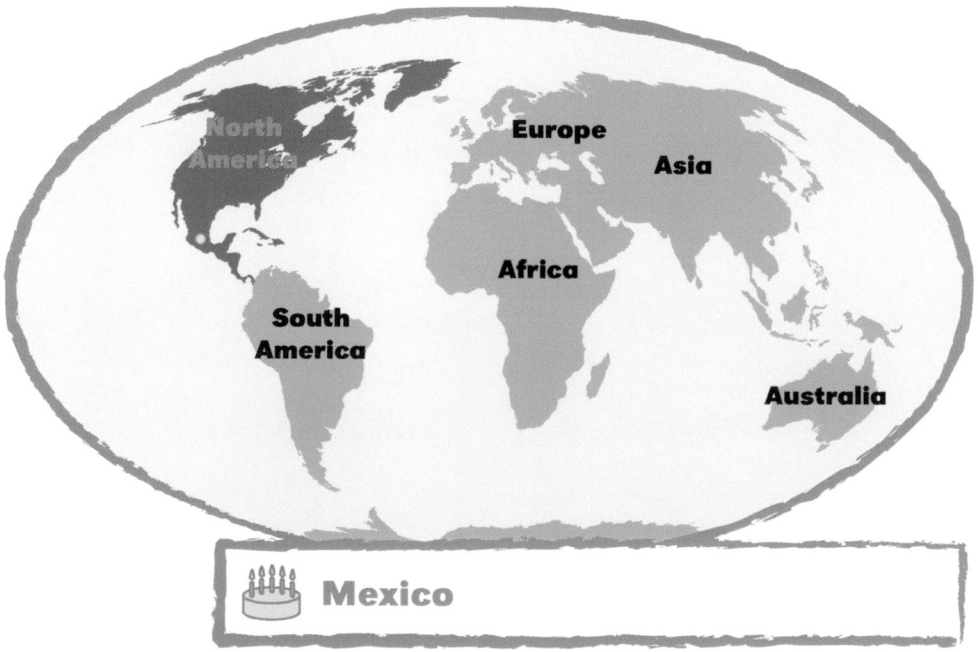

MARYL
FILM OF
RUN
THIS

A girl in the United States
bobs for apples
at her birthday party.

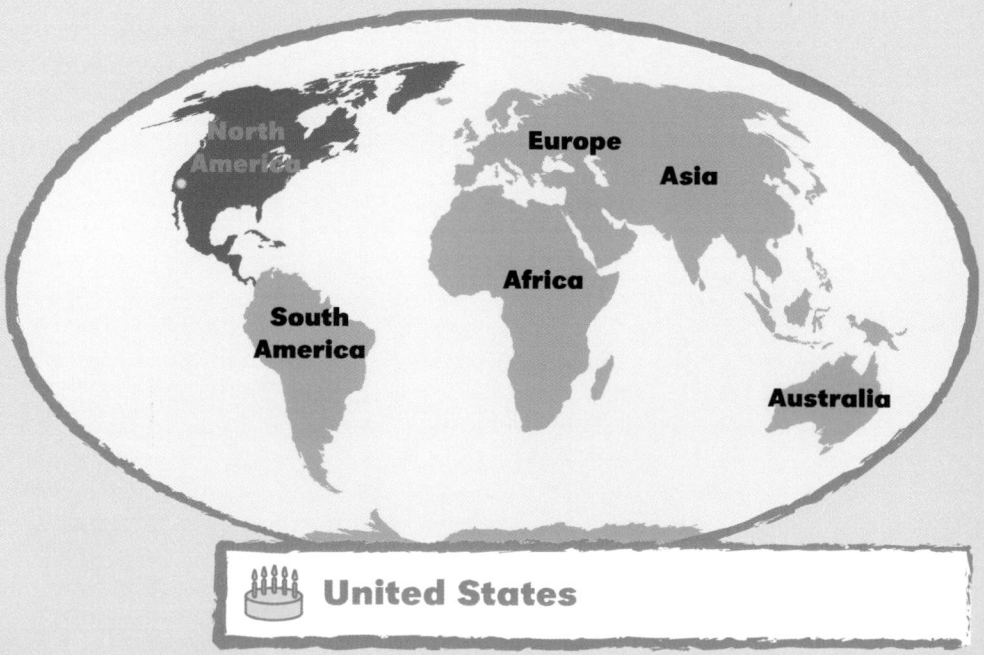

A boy in Sweden
has breakfast in bed
to celebrate his birthday.

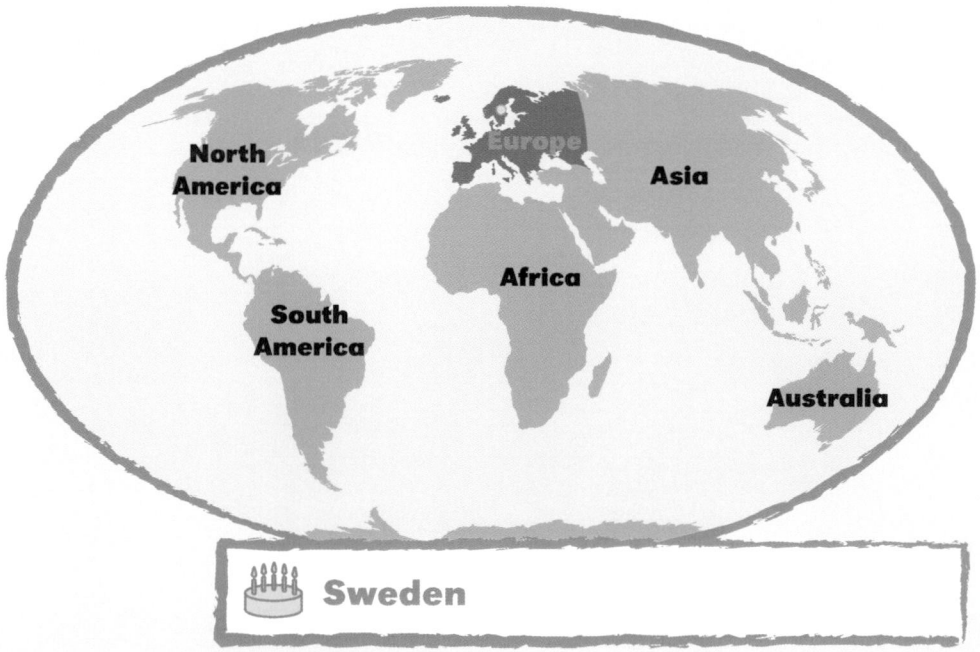

More Birthday Fun

A boy in South Africa
blows out candles
on his birthday cake.

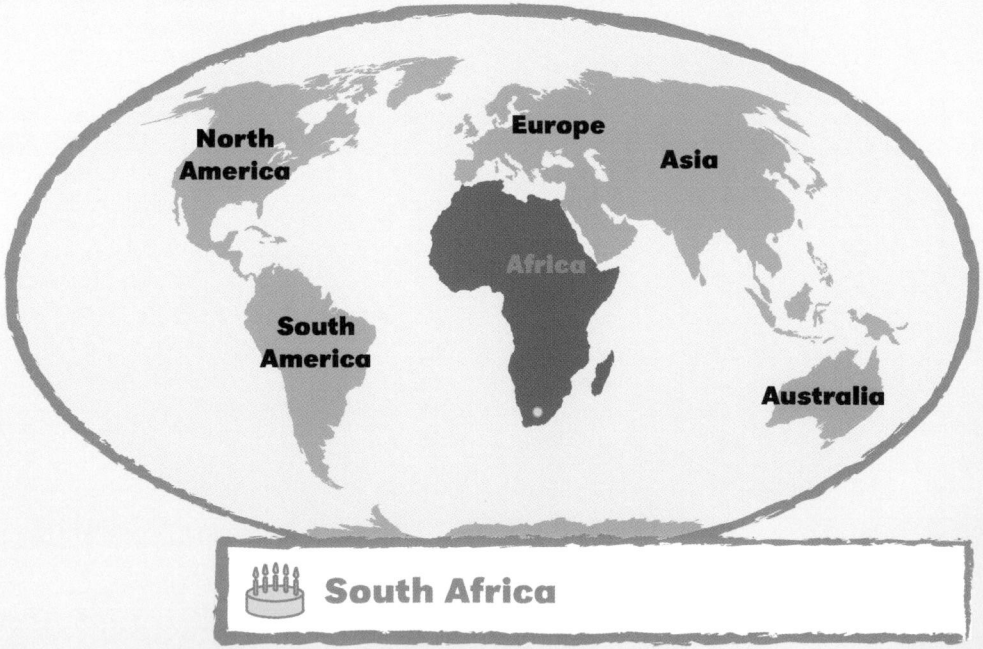

A boy in England
goes shopping
on his birthday.

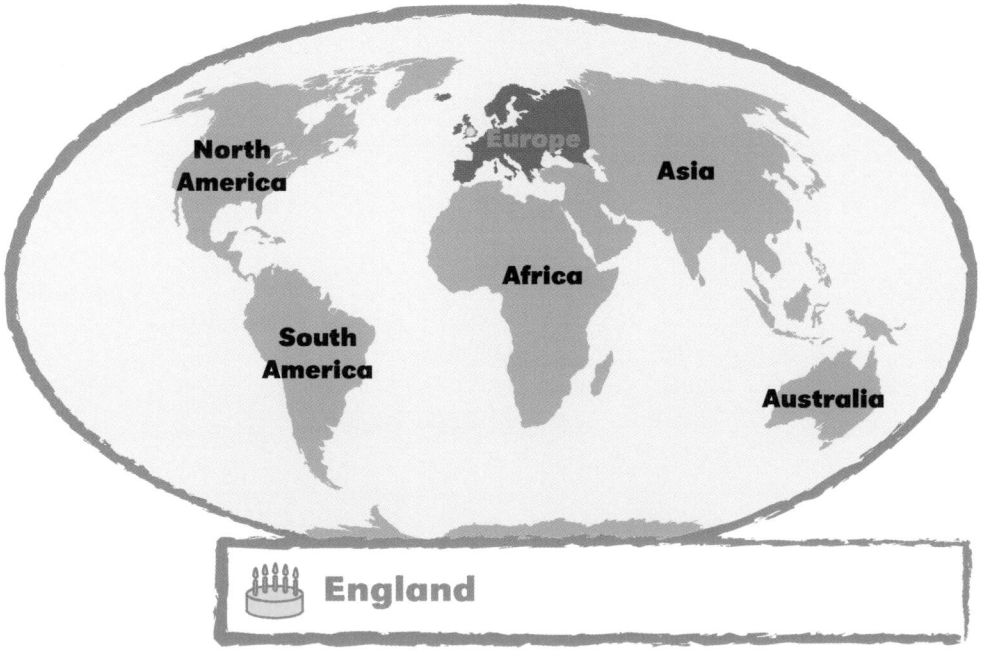

£1.50

A boy in Germany
eats at a restaurant
on his birthday.

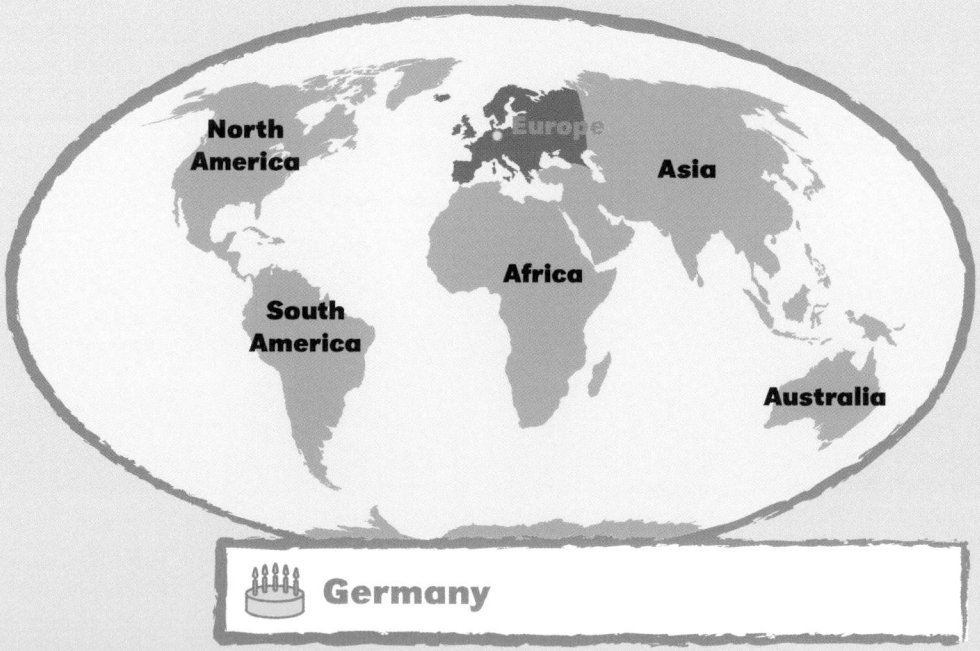

Bob
Builder

People open gifts
on their birthdays.
A girl in Mexico picks
which gift to open first.

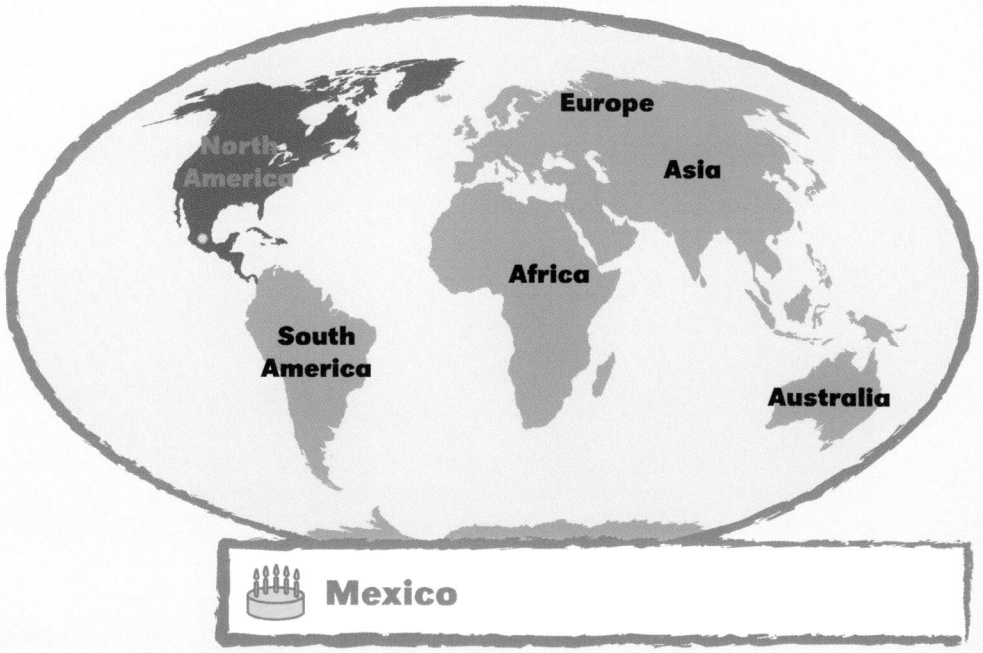

Your Birthday

Around the world,
people laugh and play
on their birthdays.
When is your birthday?

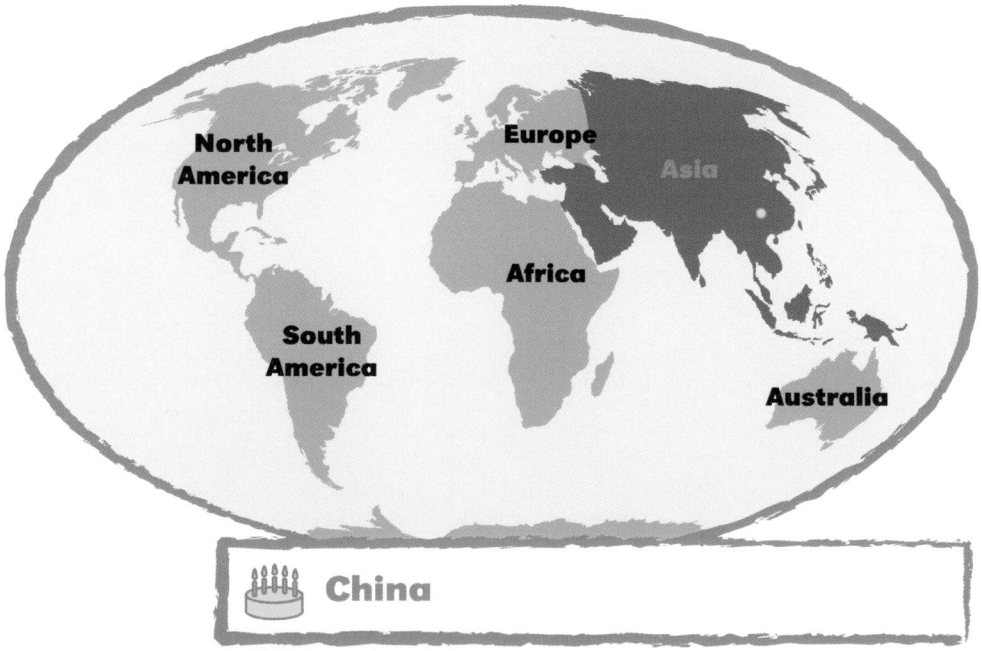

Glossary

celebrate — to do something fun, like having a party

culture — the way of life, ideas, customs, and traditions of a group of people

piñata — a container filled with candies and gifts; piñatas are popular at Latin American parties and celebrations.

restaurant — a place where people pay to eat meals

Read More

Powell, Jillian. *A Birthday.* Why Is This Day Special? North Mankato, Minn.: Smart Apple Media, 2007.

Schaefer, Ted. *When Is Your Birthday?* Science about Me. Vero Beach, Fla.: Rourke, 2007.

Stewart, Amber. *Birthday Countdown.* Columbus, Ohio: Gingham Dog Press, 2007.

Internet Sites

FactHound offers a safe, fun way to find Internet sites related to this book. All of the sites on FactHound have been researched by our staff.

Here's how:

1. Visit *www.facthound.com*
2. Choose your grade level.
3. Type in this book ID **1429617411** for age-appropriate sites. You may also browse subjects by clicking on letters, or by clicking on pictures and words.
4. Click on the **Fetch It** button.

FactHound will fetch the best sites for you!

Index

birthday cake, 12
candles, 12
cultures, 4
England, 14
games, 6, 8
Germany, 16
gifts, 18
Mexico, 6, 18
piñata, 6
restaurant, 16
shopping, 14
South Africa, 12
Sweden, 10
United States, 8

Word Count: 108
Grade: 1
Early-Intervention Level: 18